Plenty to

Gaynor Ramsey

Longman

Map of the book

Unit	Topic	Page	Lexical areas	Language actively practised	Partner work section 'You and me'
1	shopping	7	different kinds of shops; people who work in shops	**present simple** *can* + verb (1a,1b)	–
2	shopping	9	specialist shops; paying in shops	**present simple** *must* + verb (1) *like, hate, enjoy* + gerund (1)	role play interview (+ report)
3	sport	11	different sports; degrees of ability; contributors to a sporting event	**present simple** *can* + verb (1a,1b) adjectives (3)	–
4	sport	13	sports equipment; personal attitudes to sport	**present simple** *need, have to* (1b) *there is/are, have got, can,* present continuous (2)	find the differences picture interview (+ report)
5	homes	15	different kinds of homes; descriptions of homes; restrictions on homes we can have	**present simple** *I'd like, I'd prefer* (1c) *can, must* (3)	–
6	homes	17	descriptions of buildings; rooms and furniture	**present simple** prepositions of place (2)	question and answer picture description
7	jobs	19	descriptions of jobs; conditions of work	**present simple** frequency adverbs (1b) *can, will, was* (2) adjectives (3)	–
8	jobs	21	men and women's jobs; office interiors	**present simple** *there is/are, would like, have got* (2) prepositions of place (2)	interview 'What's my line?' guessing quiz find the differences picture
9	food	23	places where people eat; different kinds of food and drink; favourite food and drink; typical national food and drink	**present simple** past simple *was/were* (4)	–
10	food	25	eating in restaurants; ingredients for a recipe; different styles of food	**present and past simple** *should* (1) *have got, need* (2)	word association activity information gap – recipe
11	money	27	forms of money; being without money; children and money	**past simple** *should* (3,4)	–
12	money	29	different currencies; using money; money and travel	**present simple** present in future (2)	interview role play
13	clothes and looks	31	interpreting appearances; facial expressions; describing people's faces; uniforms	**present simple** adjectives (3)	–
14	clothes and looks	33	describing clothes; describing people; personal attitudes to clothes	**present and past simple** *couldn't* (1)	picture description interview (+ report)

Unit	Topic	Page	Lexical areas	Language actively practised	Partner work section 'You and me'
15	families and friends	35	different family structures; personal memories of family; best friends	**present and past simple** past simple *was/were* (2)	–
16	families and friends	37	relatives; family tree; special celebrations	**present simple** *have got* (1,2)	information gap – family tree
17	education	39	school traditions; personal attitudes to learning	**past simple** present continuous, *would like* (2)	–
18	education	41	school subjects; personal memories of school; language schools	**past simple** *best/worst* (2)	role play interview (+ report)
19	then and now	43	personal memories of the past	**past simple** *used to* (1,2)	–
20	then and now	45	inventions and developments; important personal past events	**past simple** *best/worst* (2)	information gap – past experiences
21	holidays	47	different kinds of holidays; describing holidays; features of hotels	**past simple** *must* + verb (3b)	–
22	holidays	49	good and bad holidays; different ways of travelling; personal travel experience	**past simple and present perfect** *can* + verb (1) comparatives (2) *have you ever* (2,3)	for and against interview
23	health	51	health risks; looking after yourself	**present simple** present continuous (1) *should* (1) imperatives (2)	–
24	health	53	parts of the body; accidents and illnesses; habits which affect health	**present perfect and past simple** *have you ever* (2) present simple (3)	interview analysis of interview
25	free time	55	entertainment; active experience in entertainment	**present perfect and past simple** *have you ever* (1) *have you ever* contrasted with past simple (1)	–
26	free time	57	hobbies; other free time activities; technology and our free time	**present simple and present perfect** *would like* (2)	interview for and against
27	plans for the future	59	future plans; an end-of-course celebration; future changes in society	**future form – going to** *would like* (1) *shall, could* (2,3)	–
28	plans for the future	61	different kinds of plans; holiday plans; short- and long-term plans	**future form – going to** present simple (1,2) *need to* (1,3)	information gap – story story retelling

To the teacher

Plenty to Say is designed to encourage elementary students to become involved in conversations – in pairs, small groups or as a class – about topics that lie within their own personal experience, or awaken their curiosity and interest.

There are twenty-eight units in the book, covering fourteen topics in all. The topics are treated from a variety of angles and the students are always asked to relate the ideas to themselves, their surroundings, their everyday lives and their pasts. Each topic covers two units and the individual purposes of these two units is a feature which is present throughout the whole book.

The first of each pair of units serves as an introduction to the topic, very often leading in with picture stimuli or a questionnaire. Following tasks make use of various group formations and can be used individually and in a different order if necessary. The tasks are purposely independent of each other so that every teacher and every class can determine the content of the lesson, according to the time available and the interests of the students, by selecting the work they want to do.

The second unit of each pair usually leads in with some vocabulary work in order to break into the topic again (probably at the beginning of a new lesson) and then very quickly changes to a section called **You and me**, which sets up a wide variety of partner activities. These activities range from role plays and interviews to word association games and information gap tasks, and the students should be given the opportunity to explore the topics together without too much guidance or intervention from the teacher. In some cases, the students are asked to report back on what they found out during this partner work phase, and in other cases the results of a conversation can be left as something known only to the two people involved. Both units in each pair finish up with a section called **Class talk** which then brings the students back into their class group to consider the topic from another angle.

WHAT SORT OF PREPARATION NEEDS TO BE DONE WITH THE STUDENTS FOR THESE ACTIVITIES?

The sort of preparation, and the time needed to do it, depends mainly on two things:
a) the students' familiarity with the vocabulary and the structures they will have to use
b) the students' experience of activities which emphasise fluency rather than accuracy, and which depend on their active participation to succeed.

If the teacher realises that necessary vocabulary is not known, then this should be pre-taught, using, wherever possible, the technique of letting the students ask for vocabulary items that they think they will need. It may be useful to focus students' attention on the structures they will need to use, and this is very often done in the units in the form of examples.

The **You and me** sections may require a bit more preparation, particularly in the units where they contain role plays or interviews. The task of carrying out a role play or an interview can seem rather daunting to an elementary-level student, but the task can be made much more approachable if the teacher carries out a sample role play or a sample interview in the class, so that the students can hear how the questions should be formed.

HOW DO THE STUDENTS ACTUALLY WORK ON THE ACTIVITIES?

Nearly all of the activities and conversations can be carried out in pairs or in small groups. If students are unused to working like this then it might take a short time for them to get used to it. They will probably very soon discover that they are able to say more and become more interested in their fellow learners by working in this way, and will learn to expect that concentrated focus on aspects of language apart from fluency takes place in another lesson or phase. Ideally, the teacher should develop a fast and effective way of dividing the class so that students work with different partners and groups as often as possible. The teacher should also often try to be a member of a group, in such a way as not to inhibit the students' interaction.

WHAT IS IN THE UNITS?

There is a Map of the book on pages 2–3. This table gives the following information:
a) the general topic of each unit
b) the lexical areas that are treated, giving an idea of the angles from which the topic is presented
c) the language that is actively practised – the item in bold print shows the main tense form that is used throughout the unit, the others are language items which occur in one or more tasks of the unit (with the number of that task given in brackets for easy reference)
d) the type of student activity that is set up in the **You and me** partner work sections – this should help the teacher to decide on the amount of preparation needed

WHAT SORT OF TASKS AND ACTIVITIES OCCUR THROUGHOUT THE BOOK?

There are some exercise types which can be found throughout the material. These are mainly identifiable by their titles. Here is a list of the activity types most often used:
a) **Pictures to talk about**: this can be found at the beginning of units and serves to introduce the topic and focus on necessary vocabulary (examples: unit 1, part 1; unit 7, part 1).
b) **Class talk**: this comes at the end of every unit and aims at bringing the students back together after working in pairs or in groups. The teacher may, however, decide to let the students discuss some of these ideas in smaller groups rather than with the class all together, particularly if the class is large.
c) **Vocabulary**: the puzzle-like activities that are included here could also be worked on by the students individually, to add variety to the styles of working. These sections occur at the beginning of the second unit on each topic.
d) **You and me**: these activities can be found in every even-numbered unit (ie. in the second unit about each topic). the pages have been designed so that partner A cannot see what partner B has got in his/her book (and vice versa). Apart from role plays and interviews, real information gap tasks are set up. In some cases the students are expected to report back on what they have talked about.
e) **A questionnaire**: this is intended as an introduction to topics, encouraging the students to share their experience first, before going on to aspects that they might have to speculate about (examples: unit 3, part 1; unit 19, part 1).
Apart from these, there are a number of other exercises which are one-off activities, with titles relating to their content (examples: An article about a job

(unit 1, part 2); There aren't only players! (unit 3, part 2); What's your flat like? (unit 5, part 2); An interview for a job (unit 7, part 2); Money in films (unit 11, part 1) and many more).

A cut-out key is available at the back of the book for closed answers.

The success of the conversations and activities prompted by the contents of *Plenty to Say* depends on a few other factors, apart from the interest level of the students in the topics. The students:

a) should be encouraged to obtain the vocabulary they need in order to say what they want

b) should be made responsible for the actual carrying out of the conversations, tasks, etc.

c) should be able to work in an atmosphere which allows them to become personally involved in what they are saying, and to consider the topics subjectively

d) should work with each other (and with the teacher as one of a group) as often as possible

e) should not be inhibited by correction during an activity (unless a serious misunderstanding has taken place because of incorrect language use)

Happy talking and listening to anyone who uses *Plenty to Say* – may your conversations be lively, demanding and interesting!

To the student

In *Plenty to Say* you can find a lot of things to talk about. You can find a lot of help and ideas, too. If you need more help (with language) or more ideas, ask your teacher. Try to say as much as you can about the topics, and try to let other students get to know you better – people are usually interested in other people! Happy talking! Happy listening!

Shopping

Pictures to talk about

A Where are the people in each of these pictures? Write A, B, C and D here:

1 _____ a record shop   2 _____ a department store
3 _____ a supermarket   4 _____ a market

What are the differences between these places? What do you think the people are buying? What else do you think they can buy here?

Useful language:
Can I . . .? Do you . . .?
How much . . .?

B Choose two of the pictures, and write two questions that the customers might ask.

Picture _____   1 _____

                     2 _____

Picture _____   1 _____

                     2 _____

Form groups of three or four. Have a look at the questions you've got in your group. Give possible answers to all these questions.

An article about a job

A You want to interview two of the people below about their jobs, for an article in a magazine. Write five questions with *do* or *does* that you plan to ask. Here are some example questions for a man who owns a small village shop.

How many days a week do you work?
Do you employ anybody to help you in the shop?
Does the shop open at the same time every day?
Where do you buy your vegetables?
What do you like best about your job?

These are the people you can choose from:

a store detective in a lady who sells fruit a young girl who works
a large department and vegetables in a in a boutique
store market

B Work with a partner. Your partner is now the store detective, the market lady or the girl, and you can ask the questions. Make a note of the answers so that you have the information for your article.

C Now write your short article.

Class talk

Choose one or two of these questions to discuss together. Tell the others in your class about your personal experiences.
- What are the things you enjoy and the things you don't enjoy about shopping for clothes?
- Do you always go shopping alone? What are the advantages and disadvantages of going with someone else?
- What differences can there be in shopping at different times of the year?

2 Shopping

PART 1

Vocabulary

You like shopping in small shops and not in large supermarkets. You want to buy the things on this list. Where must you go to buy these things? Rearrange the letters to find out.

1 **I must go to the baker's.** _____

2 _____

3 _____

4 _____

5 _____

6 _____

7 _____

☐ the mstihec's
☑ the rkbea's
☐ the tloifrs's
☐ the rroecg's
☐ the hcbutre's
☐ the eeeggocrnrr's
☐ the oirettsan's

PART 2

You and me

PARTNER A

■ **Role play** You are a customer in a bookshop:
- you want a special book about Australia
- you've only got £8.00 with you
- you've got a credit card
- your cheque book is at home
- you could go home for more money and get back to the shop just before five o'clock
- you *must* have this book
- you accept the assistant's offer of help

■ **Interview your partner** Make a note of his/her answers. Find out:
a) where he/she usually buys food
b) how often he/she goes to a market
c) what he/she likes and dislikes about department stores
d) what he/she likes buying
e) what he/she hates buying

■ Your partner has got some questions to ask you. Give plenty of information in your answers.

You and me

PARTNER B

■ **Role play** You work in a bookshop:
- you've got the book the customer wants
- the price of the book is £8.50
- you don't accept credit cards in your shop
- you accept cheques
- your shop closes at 4 pm today
- you can reserve the book for seven days if the customer pays 25% of the price
- you have to fill in a form to reserve a book

■ Your partner has got some questions to ask you. Give plenty of information in your answers.

■ **Interview your partner** Make a note of his/her answers. Find out:
1) how he/she feels about large supermarkets and shopping centres
2) what sort of shop he/she would enjoy working in
3) what sort of shop he/she would hate working in (and why)
4) which sort of shops he/she likes looking around
5) if he/she finds shopping in other countries more or less enjoyable than at home

---

Class talk

- Now make a class report on your partner A/partner B interviews.
  A: Tell the others about your partner's answers to questions d) and e).
  B: Tell the others about your partner's answers to questions 2) and 3).

- Collect the information on the blackboard like this:

He/She likes buying	He/She hates buying	He/She would enjoy working in	He/She would hate working in

- Are there any answers that are the same?

3 Sport

A questionnaire

A This is a questionnaire about sport. Ask these questions beginning with *Can you . . .?* to five people. Write down what they say like this:

***	=	yes, very well
**	=	yes, but not very well
*	=	yes, but badly
✗	=	no

If there is a sport that is very popular in your country and isn't in the questionnaire, write it in as question 10.

	Name					
1 ride a bike						
2 play ice or field hockey						
3 play tennis						
4 play table tennis						
5 swim						
6 ski						
7 play football						
8 play golf						
9 play badminton						
10						

B Write short reports about three of the sports in the questionnaire.

Example: Report on tennis:

Three of the five people can play tennis, two can play well and one can play . . . but badly.

Example: Report on football:

None of the five people can play football.

Write about 1 the sport with the most positive answers
2 the one with the most negative answers
3 the sport you like best

1 Report on _____

_____

_____

2 Report on _____

_____

_____

3 Report on _____

_____

_____

C Now choose one of these reports and read it to the rest of the class.

There aren't only players!   The people that you can see below have a special function at a football match. What do you think they have to do? Work in groups of three or four to make a sentence about each person you can see here.

Example:
1 *This woman sells programmes to the spectators when they arrive at the stadium.*

Class talk   Which sports do you think are:
• very exciting to watch?
• very boring to watch?
• very dangerous to play?
• very fast to play?
• very slow to play?
• very interesting to watch?
• very good for people who want to stay fit?

4 Sport

Vocabulary

A Which words go with which sports? Choose one word from each box for each sport.

ball   ball   ball   shuttlecock

club   racket   racket   stick

hole   goal   net   net

on a tennis court	on a golf course	on a badminton court	on a hockey field

B You need a ball and a stick to play this sport, and you have to hit the ball into the goal with a stick. Which sport is this? It's _____

C Write a short description like this about one of the other sports. Read your description to someone and ask them to write down the name of the sport.

You and me

PARTNER **A**

■ You and your partner have got almost the same picture. Talk to each other about the pictures so that you can find the eight differences. Ask questions like:

Is there a/Are there any . . .?
Where is/are . . .?
Can you see . . .?
Have you got a . . . in your picture?
How many . . . are there?
What is . . . wearing/doing . . .?

■ **Interview your partner** Make a note of his/her answers. Find out:
a) which sports he/she watches on television
b) if he/she likes football
c) if he/she ever reads the sports pages of the newspaper
d) if he/she prefers winter sports or summer sports
e) what he/she does to keep fit

■ Your partner has got some questions to ask you. Give plenty of information in your answers.

PART 2

PARTNER B

■ You and your partner have got almost the same picture. Talk to each other about the pictures so that you can find the eight differences. Ask questions like:

Is there a/Are there any . . .?
Where is/are the . . .?
Can you see . . .?
Have you got a . . . in your picture?
How many . . . are there?
What is . . . wearing/doing . . .?

■ Your partner has got some questions to ask you. Give plenty of information in your answers.

■ **Interview your partner** Make a note of his/her answers. Find out:
1) if he/she is interested in sport (actively or passively)
2) if he/she likes tennis
3) which sport he/she understands well
4) which sport he/she doesn't understand at all
5) what he/she does to keep fit

PART 3

● Now make a class report on your partner **A**/partner **B** interviews.
A: Tell the others about your partner's answers to b), d) and e). Give <u>your</u> answers to b) and d) too.
B: Tell the others about your partner's answers to 2), 3) and 5). Give <u>your</u> answers to 2) and 3) too.

● Collect the information on the blackboard like this:

Like football?		Sports		Like tennis?		Sports we understand	Keep fit
Yes	No	Summer	Winter	Yes	No		

● How many different sports can you understand well in your class?

5 Homes

Pictures to talk about

A What sort of homes are these? Write A, B, C and D here:

1 _____ a caravan   2 _____ a flat   3 _____ a house   4 _____ a houseboat

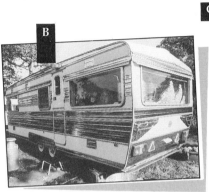

B Work with a partner and continue this list of the advantages and disadvantages of living in each of these places:

	Advantages	Disadvantages
the house	It's big there's a garden	the heating is expensive there's a lot of work to do in the garden
the caravan		
the houseboat		
the flat		

C Would you like to live in the places in the photos? Perhaps you'd like to live in one of them in the summer, but not in the winter. Or perhaps you'd like to stay in one of them for a holiday but you wouldn't like to live there all the time. Talk about the four places starting with these words:

I'd like to live/stay in . . .
I'd prefer to live/stay in . . .   } *because . . .*
I wouldn't like to live/stay in . . .

What's your flat like?

A George is talking to Anna about her home. Put Anna's part of the conversation in the correct order. George starts:

1	Where do you live, Anna?	____	Yes, of course.
2	How big is it?	____	No, it's also a bit cold there – the heating isn't very good.
3	And a kitchen and bathroom?	__1__	In a flat, near the station.
4	Are the rooms big?	____	Mm, no . . . it's quite cheap really.
5	Is it expensive?	____	I'd like to have a small house near the sea – with an orange tree in the garden.
6	And are you happy there?	____	Yes, I am – but it isn't perfect, you know.
7	Oh? What's wrong with it then?	____	The living room is, but the bedroom's a bit small. But it's okay.
8	Is that all?	____	It's got two rooms.
9	Where would you really like to live?	____	Well, there's a lot of traffic in the street outside – so it's a bit noisy.

B Read the dialogue between George and Anna with a partner. Then go through it again – one person reading George's questions, and the other person giving <u>real</u> answers, not Anna's answers.

Class talk

The 'Homes for Everyone' Society would like to make some new rules about houses and flats. Decide for yourself if you think these rules are good or bad and then discuss your decisions and reasons with the rest of your class.

	Good	Bad
• People with dogs or cats can't live in flats.	☐	☐
• Single people must live in small flats (maximum 2 rooms).	☐	☐
• Young people must live with their parents until they are 25, get married or go away to university.	☐	☐
• All university students can live free in accommodation paid for by the government.	☐	☐
• Parents must move if their children leave home and their house or flat is larger than necessary for two people.	☐	☐

6 Homes

Vocabulary

Match these jumbled words to the drawings of the outside and the inside of a house.

1 nwdiwo _____

2 oofr _____

3 psstuiar _____

4 odor _____

5 caitt _____

6 rssita _____

7 lalw _____

8 ymnhiec _____

9 sdnsrotawi _____

the outside

a)
b)
c)
d)
e)

the inside

f)
g)
h)
i)

You and me

PARTNER A

■ Ask your partner these questions. Are his/her answers positive or negative?

Do you live in a house with a garden?	+	−
Do you live with more than two other people?	+	−
Is your furniture extremely modern?	+	−
Do you live less than twenty kilometres from an airport?	+	−
Have you got a garage?	+	−
Is your house too small for you?	+	−
Are you the owner of your home?	+	−
Is your home in a big city?	+	−

How many negative answers have you got? _____

Go back to the negative answers and ask another question.
Example: If the first answer is negative you can now ask:
You don't live in a house with a garden – well, do you live in a house without a garden or in a flat?

■ Your partner is going to ask you eight questions now. Just answer *yes* or *no*.

■ Tell your partner where the furniture is in Room 2.

A = dining table and chairs   B = coffee table   C = armchair
D = sofa   E = television   F = music centre   G = bookcase

Useful language: *in the northwest corner, across the corner, between, next to, opposite, on the east wall, behind*

■ Your partner is going to tell you where the furniture is in Room 1. Draw the furniture in.

■ Which of these two rooms do you and your partner think is the best?

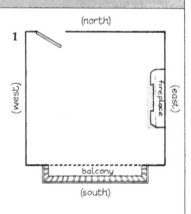

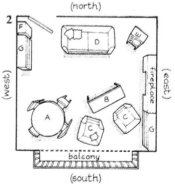

PART 2

You and me

PARTNER B

■ Your partner is going to ask you eight questions. Just answer *yes* or *no*.

■ Ask your partner these questions. Are his/her answers positive or negative?

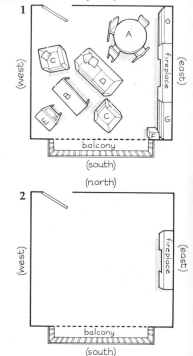

Do you live in a small village?	+	–
Is your home very near a station?	+	–
Do you live alone?	+	–
Has your home got three bedrooms?	+	–
Is your home on more than one floor?	+	–
Has your home got any disadvantages?	+	–
Do you like all the furniture you've got?	+	–
Have you got a balcony?	+	–

How many negative answers have you got? _____

Go back to the negative answers and ask another question.
Example: If the first answer is negative you can now ask:
You don't live in a small village – well, how big is the place where you live?

■ Your partner is going to tell you where the furniture is in Room 2. Draw the furniture in.

A = dining table and chairs   B = coffee table   C = armchair
D = sofa   E = television   F = music centre   G = bookcase

■ Tell your partner where the furniture is in Room 1.

Useful language: *in the northeast corner, across the corner, between, next to, opposite, on the east wall, behind.*

■ Which of these two rooms do you and your partner think is the best?

PART 3

Class talk

What are typical homes like in your country?
- Talk about the rooms, the heating, the outside of the building, etc.
- Compare homes in your country with homes in another country where they are different. How (and why) are they different?

7 Jobs

Pictures to talk about

A Look at these pictures of people working. Match the correct picture to the name of the job.

1 _____ taxi driver   2 _____ singer   3 _____ policeman
4 _____ air hostess   5 _____ teacher   6 _____ gardener

A   B   C

D   E   F

B Which of the jobs do you think these words go with?

regular working hours: _____   inside: _____

uniform: _____   noisy: _____

alone: _____   dangerous: _____

away from home: _____   dirty: _____

Discuss your decisions with someone else.

Talk about all six jobs using the following words:

I expect he/she often . . .   *I'm sure he/she always has to . . .*
He/She is lucky because . . .   *I hope he/she never . . .*
It must be awful to have to . . .   *I expect he/she is happy . . .*

C Now choose one of the jobs and finish these sentences for that job.

Job: _____

I expect _____ often _____

I'm sure _____ always has to _____

_____ is lucky because _____

I hope _____ never _____

It must be awful to have to _____

I expect _____ is happy _____

PART 2

An interview for a job

A The woman you can see in this picture is interviewing the young man for a job. She's the manageress of a hotel in a seaside holiday resort. The job that the young man would like to have is a summer job at the reception desk of the hotel. Both the interviewer (the woman) and the interviewee (the young man) have got several questions to ask. Work together with a partner to form these questions.

The interviewer would like to know how old the man is.

How old are you?

_____

She would also like to know if the young man can speak French or Italian.

_____

_____

She needs to know if he can type. She wants to know if he can drive.

_____

_____

She'd like to know who his last employer was.

_____

_____

She wants to know what his last job was.

_____

_____

The manageress wants to know if he can start next Saturday.

_____

_____

The young man would like to know how many people the hotel employs.

_____

_____

He'd like to know if he will sometimes have to work at night.

_____

_____

He wants to know how many hours a week he'll have to work.

_____

_____

He wants to know how many free days he'll have.

_____

_____

He needs to know if he can have a room in the hotel.

_____

_____

He wants to know what his salary will be.

_____

_____

B Now take the parts of the interviewer and interviewee and ask and answer the questions you have prepared.

PART 3

Class talk

Which jobs in your country do you think are:
- very exciting?
- very boring?
- very dirty?

- very well paid?
- very glamorous?
- very dangerous?

8 Jobs

Vocabulary

Three of the words below change and end in 'ess', if the person doing the job is a woman. Two of the others change in a different way, and three don't change at all! Write in the words for a woman who does these jobs:

Man	Woman	Man	Woman
teacher	_____	shop manager	_____
policeman	_____	salesman	_____
actor	_____	waiter	_____
taxi driver	_____	singer	_____

Compare your list with others in your class.

PART 2

You and me

PARTNER A

■ **Interview your partner** Find out if your partner's got a job.

If the answer is *yes*, find out
a) what his/her job is
b) if there is anything about the job he/she doesn't enjoy
c) what hours he/she works
d) some details about his/her place of work (factory/office etc.)
e) about the people he/she works with

If the answer is *no*, find out
a) why he/she hasn't got a job
b) what job he/she would like to have
c) if there is a job he/she wouldn't like to do
d) if he/she would like to work full time or part time
e) what his/her parents' jobs are/were

■ Think of a job (not your real job, something very different), but don't tell your partner what that job is. Your partner is going to ask you a maximum of fifteen questions to try and find out what job you're thinking about. You can only answer *yes* or *no*.
Example: If your partner asks *Do you work outdoors?* you can only answer *Yes, I do* or *No, I don't.*

■ You and your partner have got almost the same picture. Talk to each other about the pictures so that you can find the ten differences. Ask questions like:

How many . . . are there?
Where's the . . .?
What is/are the . . . like?
Have you got a . . . in your picture?
Is/Are the . . . next to/on/under the . . .?

PART 2

PARTNER B

■ Your partner has got some questions to ask you. Give plenty of information in your answers.

■ **Interview your partner** Your partner is thinking of a job (not his/her real job). You can ask a maximum of fifteen questions, and try to find out what the job is. Your partner can only answer *yes* or *no*. Start with these questions. Find out:

1 if he/she works inside or outdoors
  Example: You can ask *Do you work outdoors?* and your partner will answer *Yes, I do* or *No, I don't*.
2 if he/she works alone or with others (You can ask *Do you work alone?*)
3 if he/she handles money as part of the job
4 if he/she uses the phone a lot
5 if he/she stands or sits most of the time
Now go on – you've got ten more questions, and then you can ask:
Are you a . . .?

■ You and your partner have got almost the same picture. Talk to each other about the pictures so that you can find the ten differences. Ask questions like:

How many . . . are there?
Where is/are the . . .?
What is/are the . . . like?
Have you got a . . . in your picture?
Is/are the . . . next to/on/under the . . .?

PART 3

What is the work situation like in your country?
● Are a lot of people out of work?
● What help can a person get if he/she hasn't got a job?
● How do people try to find jobs?
● Do married women usually work?

9 Food

Pictures to talk about

A Here are four photographs of people who are eating something – none of them are at home.

Where are the people in the pictures? Write A, B, C and D here:

1 _____ in a canteen   2 _____ in a field or park

3 _____ in the street   4 _____ in an expensive restaurant

B Talk about the differences between the places, the food, the cost and the comfort of A, B, C and D. Do you ever eat in places like these? Where do you usually eat?

PART 2

Vocabulary

Write two examples of food or drink in each of these boxes:

Vegetables	Fruit

Fish	Meat

Now compare your words with a partner, and write in any different ones he/she has got.
Do the same in a group of four. How many words have you got in each box now?

PART 3

You and me

A Talk to your partner about food, and make a list for both of you.

	Me	My partner
• your favourite food		
• something to eat that you don't like		
• a drink that you don't like		
• a national speciality that you like		
• your speciality (as a cook!)		

B What do you think is typical food and drink from these countries?

Spain _____   England _____

Italy _____   America _____

Greece _____   India _____

China _____   Mexico _____

Compare with a different partner.

PART 4

Class talk

Tell the others five facts about the last breakfast, lunch or dinner you had.
(What? Where? Who with? etc.)

PART 1

Vocabulary

These twelve words could be used to describe the food, the service and the inside of a restaurant. Divide them into three groups of four words, using each word only once.

slow   attractive   friendly   interesting   modern   awful   elegant
over-cooked   unfriendly   shabby   excellent   fast

The food	The service	The inside of the restaurant

Which of these words say something positive about the restaurant, and which say something negative? Which do you think is the most positive and the most negative word in each group? Are there any words here that could be put in all three groups?

PART 2

You and me

PARTNER A

■ Say these words to your partner one by one. Your partner will instantly say the first word he/she thinks of.
Example: You say *milk* and he/she says *cow*, *cheese* or *butter*. Write down the word your partner says:

soup _____   hamburger _____

Chinese food _____   breakfast _____

drink _____   vegetables _____

meat _____   picnic _____

■ Your partner has got some words for you, too. Do the same thing and he/she will write down what you say.

■ Here is a list of the things you need to make fish pie. Your partner wants to make fish pie this evening but he/she hasn't got a shopping list and can't remember all the things. You're on the phone now. Can you help your partner. Spell the words so he/she can write them down. It doesn't matter if you or your partner don't understand what all these things are. He/she can ask in the shop.

225g cod or haddock
salt
black pepper
milk
1 tin of pimiento
dried dill
1 egg
fresh parsley
20g butter or margarine
20g plain flour
350g potatoes
25g Cheddar cheese

You and me

PARTNER *B*

■ Your partner is going to say eight words to you one by one. Say the first word you think of in reply.
Example: Your partner says *milk* and you could say *cow, cheese* or *butter*.

■ Now you can do the same. Write down the words your partner says:

snack _____ traditional food _____

Indian food _____ fish _____

expensive food _____ slimmer's food _____

dessert _____ health food _____

■ You are in the town centre. You want to cook fish pie this evening but you haven't got a shopping list. You're on the phone to your partner who is at home. Find out which things you need to buy. Your partner can spell the difficult words for you.

At home you've got:	In your shopping bag you've got:	You need to buy:
salt	*haddock*	_____
white pepper	*a tin of pimiento*	_____
plain flour	*1 kg potatoes*	_____
Parmesan cheese	*dried parsley*	_____
butter	*a bottle of milk*	_____

PART *3*

Class talk

Talk about the food and ways of cooking that are popular in your country. If you are all from the same country, tell each other about your experiences of food in other countries.

11 Money

Money in films

The comments about money that you can see below all come from film dialogues. Work in groups of three or four to decide:
1 what the film was about
2 who spoke these words
3 who listened to these words in the film

a) 66 Oh, no . . . you mean that we've got nothing left, nothing at all. It's all gone! What are we going to do? 99

b) 66 Look, lady . . . just give me the money, keep quiet and you'll be fine . . . just fine. 99

c) 66 Okay, here's the money. Now leave me alone, let me live my life – don't make me pay any more, I've paid you enough. 99

d) 66 I can't give you any money – I haven't got any more to give you. You need help . . . more money isn't going to help you at all. 99

Compare your ideas with the others in your class.

PART 2

Vocabulary

What forms of money are these? You need these letters to finish the words:

a d d e e e e h i i n o o q r r s t t u

1

2   BANK   1 · 12 · 1931
      Pay Cash   or order
      Ten Pounds only   £10 00
                         MR. J. SMITH
                         J. Smith
      403102 91 012575 10356285

3   BANK OF ENGLAND
      TEN
      POUNDS

4   CREDIT CARD
      9031 43 709
      MR. J. SMITH

1 c_____   2 c_____   3 £10 n_____   4 c_____ c_____

Which two of these four are also called cash? _____ and _____

Which of these two have you got with you at the moment? _____

Which of these do you normally use? _____

Which of these do you prefer when you travel? _____

27

The man with no money!

A This man says he hasn't got any money, and there are several reasons why he hasn't got any money:

1 he doesn't work (he's too lazy)
2 he lives in an expensive flat in the best part of town
3 he gambles
4 he smokes a lot of big cigars
5 he's got three cars – one old Rolls Royce, one sports car and one family car

What do you think he should do?
Example:
I think he should look for a job.
I think he should work more.
I think he shouldn't be so lazy.
Suggest three ways he could solve his other problems. Use the words *should* and *shouldn't* as often as you can.

B Work with a partner to think of three more possible reasons why this man hasn't got any money:

6 _____
7 _____
8 _____

C Read your reasons to the class and listen to their ideas about what he should do to help himself.

Class talk

Decide for yourself if you agree or disagree with these statements.

	Agree	Disagree
• Children should get money for doing jobs at home.	☐	☐
• All children should have pocket money to spend how they want.	☐	☐
• Children should learn how to save and how to budget.	☐	☐
• Children shouldn't play games where the aim is to make money.	☐	☐

Discuss your decisions with the other people in your class.
Tell the others about the experiences you had with money when you were a child.

12 Money

PART 1

Vocabulary

Work in groups of four. Which of these countries do you think have 'dollars', 'francs', 'pesos' and 'pounds' as their currency. There are five in each currency group.

Australia, Belgium, Bolivia, Britain, Canada, Columbia, Congo, Cuba, Cyprus, Egypt, France, Gibraltar, Luxembourg, Malta, Mexico, New Zealand, Philippines, Singapore, Switzerland, USA

Dollars	Francs	Pesos	Pounds

PART 2

You and me

PARTNER A

■ **Interview your partner** Find out:
a) if he/she ever uses cheques
b) what form of money he/she takes abroad
c) if he/she would like to work in a bank
d) if he/she prefers gold or silver
e) if he/she knows what it is like to be poor
f) where he/she got money from when at school

■ Your partner has got some questions to ask you. Give plenty of information in your answers.

■ **Role play** You're a cashier in a bank. You're speaking to a customer at the counter:
• greet the customer and offer to help
• help the customer to decide about the amount of money he/she needs
• find out if the customer has got a credit card for hotel bills, etc. – you think this is the best method of paying for things abroad
• write down the currencies and the amounts that the customer wants
• tell the customer to come back tomorrow morning
• offer to have the money ready five minutes before closing time today (opening times 10 am to 4 pm)

You and me

PARTNER **B**

■ Your partner has got some questions to ask you. Give plenty of information in your answers.

■ **Interview your partner** Find out:
1) how much money he/she is carrying today
2) when he/she last changed money from one currency to another
3) if he/she usually pays in shops in cash, by cheque or by credit card
4) how he/she saves money
5) how often he/she goes to the bank
6) how he/she pays regular bills

■ **Role play** You're a customer in a bank. You're speaking to a cashier at the counter:
● return the cashier's greeting
● you want some travellers' cheques in US dollars
● you want some Swiss francs and German marks in cash
● you're going to Switzerland for three days
● you're going to Germany for a week
● you haven't got a credit card, you don't like them and you don't want to have one
● you're leaving this town this evening
● you don't know what time the bank closes

PART 3

Class talk

There are a lot of different things that people sometimes do with money. Most people earn money, spend money, borrow money or lend money to someone. People sometimes do these things:
● waste money
● save money
● steal money
● gamble with money.
Think of as many possible ways as you can that people sometimes do these things.

13 Clothes and looks

PART 1

Pictures to talk about

When we see people we often think that we know something about them just by their appearance. Look at these pictures. What can you say about the people after looking at the photographs?

Useful language:
He/She looks . . .
I'm sure he/she . . .
I bet he/she . . .

PART 2

Faces, faces

A Work with a partner. Draw four faces on a piece of paper, like this but bigger:

(L) with a nose in the middle.

Now choose a pair of eyes with eyebrows and a mouth to make your faces look:
a) sad   b) happy   c) surprised   d) angry.

B Now you and your partner should think of four very short stories to explain why your four people are feeling the way they are.

C Tell these stories to two other people and listen to their explanations too. Choose which of their stories you like the best.

PART 3

Vocabulary

A What does he look like? What does she look like? Match the drawings below to the adjectives on the right, by writing the numbers in the boxes.

hair: 1 2 3

☐ long and straight

☐ short and curly

☐ shoulder-length and wavy

nose: 1 2 3

☐ bent

☐ straight

☐ turned up

face: 1 2 3

☐ round

☐ square

☐ oval

some other useful words:
1 2 3

☐ glasses

☐ beard

☐ moustache

Some possible hair colours:

    white grey blond fair light brown
    brunette dark brown black

Some possible eye colours:

    grey blue green brown
    hazel

What colour is your hair? _____

What colour are your eyes? _____

B Work with a partner and write a description of his/her face and head.

C Now mix up all the papers in your class, and each person should take one. Make sure you haven't got the description you wrote *or* the description of you. Listen to the descriptions one by one and write down the names of the people whose descriptions you think they are.
Compare results in the class. How many descriptions were recognised by everybody? Was there a description that nobody recognised?

PART 4

Class talk

Some people have to wear uniforms – often because of their jobs, but sometimes for other reasons.

• Make a list of people who wear uniforms:

People who wear uniforms for their jobs	People who wear uniforms for other reasons

• Which uniforms are often attractive, and which are sometimes unattractive?
• What do you think could be the advantages and disadvantages of wearing a uniform every day?

14 Clothes and looks

❝ I went shopping for some clothes yesterday. I wanted to buy a pullover, a raincoat, a pair of shoes and a skirt. But everything I tried on was wrong . . . too big or too small or there was something else wrong. In the end, I didn't buy anything. ❞

Find the opposites of these adjectives in the box (the letters of the words are jumbled). Work with someone else if you want.

1 big **small**	5 ordinary _____
2 wide _____	6 casual _____
3 long _____	7 expensive _____
4 heavy _____	8 old-fashioned _____

htlgi	epahc
~~lsalm~~	pclaise
mnrdoe	geetnal
trosh	rraonw

Use these adjectives to talk about the things she tried on.
Example: She tried on a pullover but it was too big. She really wanted a smaller one.

PARTNER **A**

■ Describe the woman below to your partner. If there are any words you don't know or can't remember, ask your partner for help.

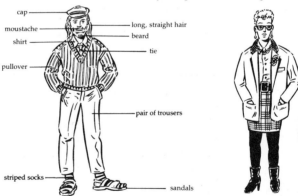

■ Your partner is going to describe the man above. You've got the necessary words here, so if your partner can't remember a word, please help. Make sure that all the words that you can see here are used.

■ **Interview your partner** Make notes of his/her answers. Find out:
a) if he/she really likes the clothes he/she is wearing today
b) what sort of clothes he/she finds comfortable
c) what sort of clothes he/she finds uncomfortable
d) what his/her favourite colour for clothes is
e) how he/she feels about shopping for clothes
f) how far he/she follows fashion

■ Your partner has got some questions to ask you. Give plenty of information in your answers.

PART 2

PARTNER B

■ Your partner is going to describe the woman below. You've got the necessary words here, so if your partner can't remember a word, please help. Make sure that all the words that you can see here are used.

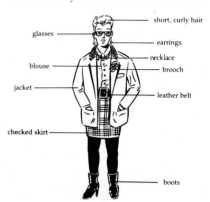

short, curly hair
glasses
earrings
necklace
blouse
brooch
jacket
leather belt
checked skirt
boots

■ Now describe the man above to your partner. If there are any words you don't know or can't remember, ask your partner for help.

■ Your partner has got some questions to ask you. Give plenty of information in your answers.

■ **Interview your partner** Make a note of his/her answers. Find out:
1) what his/her newest item of clothing is
2) if he/she likes wearing jewellery
3) if he/she likes wearing perfume
4) where he/she usually buys clothes
5) if he/she ever buys secondhand clothes
6) what his/her biggest problem is when buying clothes

PART 3

● Make a report on your partner A/partner B interviews.
A: Tell the others about your partner's answers to questions b) and c). Give your answers to these questions too.
B: Tell the others about your partner's answers to questions 1) and 5). Give your answers to these questions too.

● Collect the information on the blackboard like this:

Comfortable clothes	Uncomfortable clothes	Newest item	Secondhand clothes	
			Yes	No

15 Families and friends

Opinions

A These two children come from very different families. Here's what they think about their family situations.

❝ I'm an only child, so I'm often with adults – my parents or their friends. I can sometimes do things with them that other children can't do. Both my parents work and so I get more pocket money than children in larger families. I usually invite my friends from school to come on holiday with us. ❞

❝ My family is very big – there are six children, our parents and my grandmother all in one house. I have to share a bedroom with two sisters, and we really enjoy that. Big families are fun, you can't get lonely, that's for sure. We girls share our clothes, and we usually share one big birthday party, too. ❞

B Can you understand the way these two children feel? Work in groups of four to find as many advantages and disadvantages as you can in the situation of the only child, and as many advantages and disadvantages as you can in the situation of the girl from the large family.

Only child		Large family	
Advantages	**Disadvantages**	**Advantages**	**Disadvantages**

Now present your ideas to the others. Each person in the group can take one of the lists and present it like this:

Example:
(only child – advantages) *I'm an only child and I'm happy that I haven't got any brothers or sisters. My parents pay all their attention to me and they give me . . .* and so on.

PART **2**

Family memories

Ask these questions to one person in your class and make a note of all his/her answers.

_____'s answers:

How many children, including you, were there in your family?	
Were you the oldest child, the youngest child or somewhere in the middle?	
What was the age difference between the oldest child and the youngest?	
What do you think is an ideal number of children to have in a family?	
What was an advantage of your position in the family?	
What was a disadvantage of your position in the family?	
Did you grow up with both your parents and all your brothers and sisters?	

Look at the answers that you've got from your partner and compare them with the answers he/she has got from you. How many of your answers were the same? How similar were your families? Talk about the similarities and the differences together.

PART **3**

Class talk

Read these two comments about friends. They both come from songs.
'A boy's best friend is his mother' and 'Diamonds are a girl's best friend.'

• What do you think these comments mean?
• What can you remember about the best friend you had when you were a child?
• What 'functions' do you think best friends have when you're adult?

16 Families and friends

Vocabulary

A Write these words in the correct box below. They are all members of a family.

brother	daughter-in-law	sister-in-law	wife	grandmother	sister
cousin	grandfather	granddaughter	mother	daughter	nephew
uncle	father-in-law	son-in-law	niece	grandson	father
son	brother-in-law	mother-in-law	aunt	husband	

Female relatives	**Male relatives**

B Write a number next to each of the words to show how many relatives you've got in your family. Compare numbers with a partner.

PART 2

You and me

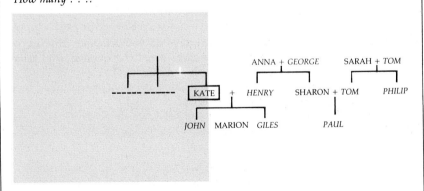

PARTNER A

■ Here is part of Kate's family tree. Your partner has got the other part. Ask questions to find out who the other twelve people are, and complete the tree. (The names in *italics* are all men's names.)
Ask questions like: *Has Kate got any brothers or sisters? What are their names? How many . . .?*

■ Now answer your partner's questions so that he/she can complete the family tree too.

■ Work with your partner to decide how these people are related to Kate. Your partner has got some names too.

Example: Marion   *She's Kate's daughter.*
a) Patty   b) David   c) Charles   d) Mike   e) Emma

PART 2

PARTNER B

■ Here is part of Kate's family tree. Your partner has got the other part, and is going to ask you questions about the information you've got. (The names in *italics* are all men's names.)

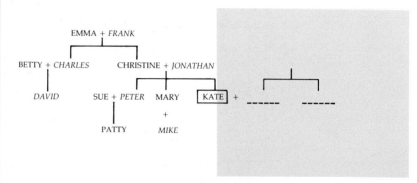

■ Now ask your partner questions about Kate's family so that you can find out who the other twelve people in the family are.

Ask questions like: *Has Kate got a husband? What's his name? How many . . .?*

■ Work with your partner to decide how these people are related to Kate. Your partner has got some names too.

Example: Mary   *She's Kate's sister.*

1) Sharon   2) Paul   3) Anna and George   4) Henry   5) Betty

PART 3

What special days do you celebrate in your country?
- Are these days usually celebrated with relatives or with friends?
- How are they celebrated?
- What about more personal special days such as birthdays and wedding anniversaries?
- How do you celebrate those days?

17 Education

Schooldays in England

A Here are six comments about school in England. Work in groups of four or five, and discuss each comment. You can see a grid under the comments – fill in the number of people in your group who can make the same comments as these about themselves, and the number who say that things were different for them.

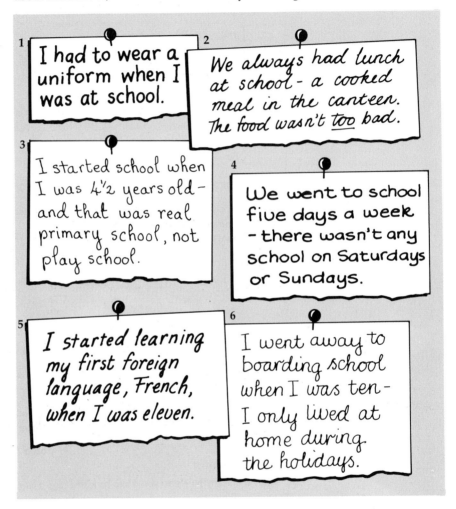

1. I had to wear a uniform when I was at school.

2. We always had lunch at school - a cooked meal in the canteen. The food wasn't too bad.

3. I started school when I was 4½ years old - and that was real primary school, not play school.

4. We went to school five days a week - there wasn't any school on Saturdays or Sundays.

5. I started learning my first foreign language, French, when I was eleven.

6. I went away to boarding school when I was ten - I only lived at home during the holidays.

COMMENT:	1	2	3	4	5	6
It was like this for me when I was at school.						
It was different for me when I was at school.						

B If any of these things were different for you, what do you think the advantages and disadvantages of the system in England could be?

You and learning

How do you feel about learning now? Answer these questions for yourself and then ask at least two other people what their answers are. Talk about the differences in your answers.

I Is English the only subject you're learning now?

☐ yes

☐ no   What other subject(s) are you learning? _____

_____

2 Is this your first experience in learning a foreign language?

☐ yes

☐ no   Where and what did you learn before? _____

_____

3 Why are you learning English? (you can choose more than one here, if you want)

☐ because I want to

☐ because I have to

☐ for my work

☐ to take an examination

☐ for my studies

☐ for my holidays

☐ because I like it

☐ because there's an English-speaker in my family or who is a friend

☐ to understand books, films or songs better

☐ other (what?) _____

4 Is there anything else you'd like to learn? (e.g. a language, a hobby or a skill)

☐ no

☐ yes   What would you like to learn? _____

Class talk

Make a list together (on the blackboard) of all the ways in which you can learn something new at your age in your country/countries. Think about:
• various types of schools
• learning by correspondence
• learning from the radio, etc.

18 Education

PART 1

Vocabulary

Here are some of the school subjects that English secondary school pupils usually have at school. Can you work out what they are?

1 t h i s o y r   H _ _ _ _ _ Y   6 s a a t c m h m e i t   M _ _ _ _ _ _ _ _ _ S

2 n f h c e r   F _ _ _ _ H   7 p g g y o a e r h   G _ _ _ _ _ _ _ Y

3 p i s s h y c   P _ _ _ _ _ S   8 y m t r h c e i s   C _ _ _ _ _ _ _ Y

4 s m c i u   M _ _ _ C   9 o o y c k r e   C _ _ _ _ Y

5 h e s g n l i   E _ _ _ _ _ H   10 t u m c p r e o   C _ _ _ _ _ _ R studies

PART 2

You and me

PARTNER A

■ **Interview your partner** Make a note of his/her answers. Find out:
a) at what age he/she started school
b) when he/she finished school
c) what types of school he/she attended
d) when he/she had to take examinations
e) about his/her best memory of school
f) about his/her worst memory of school

■ Your partner has got some questions to ask you. Give plenty of information in your answers.

■ **Role play** You're the secretary at a language school. You're talking on the phone to someone who wants to take a language course.
• get the necessary information to complete this form
• you only have classes on Mondays to Fridays
• you've got three classes at the correct level for the person on the phone:
Tuesday and Thursday 6–7.30 pm
Wednesday 7–9 pm
Wednesday and Friday 5.30–7 pm
• one of your teachers gives private lessons but only to people who are already in one of your classes

Can you help the person on the phone?

SURNAME: ....

FIRST NAME(S) ....

....

ADDRESS: ....

....

PHONE NUMBER: ....

LANGUAGE REQUIRED:

☐ English ☐ French

☐ German ☐ Spanish

☐ Italian ☐ ....

LEVEL: ☐ beginner

☐ intermediate

☐ advanced

REASON FOR LEARNING:

☐ business

☐ examination

☐ personal

PART **2**

PARTNER **B**

- ■ Your partner has got some questions to ask you. Give plenty of information in your answers.

- ■ **Interview your partner** Make a note of his/her answers. Find out:
1) what his/her favourite subject at school was
2) which subject he/she hated most
3) some information about the school he/she attended as a teenager
4) his/her opinion of teaching as a job
5) what his/her earliest memory of school is
6) if he/she still has contact with schoolfriends from the past

- ■ **Role play** You want some information about a language course. You're on the phone to a language school that has daytime and evening courses. You work full time and already have some regular evening arrangements.
  - you want to learn Spanish before your next holiday
  - you're a complete beginner
  - you'd like to go to school on Saturday mornings for three hours
  - you definitely want three hours a week
  - you definitely can't change your discussion group on Thursdays
  - if really necessary, you could change your tennis lesson to 8 pm

MONDAY:

TUESDAY: *tennis 6-7*

WEDNESDAY:

THURSDAY: *discussion 7-10*

FRIDAY: *work ?*

  - you don't want to go to school on Fridays because you sometimes have to work late
  - ask if they give private lessons at this school

Are you going to learn Spanish at this school?

PART **3**

- • Now make a class report on your partner A/partner B interviews.
A: Tell the others about your partner's answers to e) and f).
B: Tell the others about your partner's answers to 1) and 2).

- • Collect the information on the blackboard like this:

Best memory	Worst memory	Favourite subject	Most hated subject

- • A: Now answer questions e) and f) yourself, and add this new information to the report.
- • B: Answer questions 1) and 2) yourself, and complete the class report. Was English anybody's favourite or most hated subject?

Then and now

A questionnaire

A This is the beginning of a questionnaire about what people used to do when they were children, between six and ten years old. Work with two or three other people to add six more questions.

Name					
1 Did you use to live in the town where you live now?					
2 Did you use to go to school on Saturdays?					
3 Did you use to have birthday parties?					
4 Did you use to visit your grandmother or grandfather?					
5					
6					
7					
8					
9					
10					

B Now ask these questions to five people – if possible they should be five people who didn't work on the questions with you. Fill in their answers with a tick (√) or a cross (×).

C Choose the two most interesting questions on the questionnaire and write a short report about the results. Add some information about yourself to each report.

Example: **Report on question 1:**

Two people used to live in the town where they live now, and the other three used to live in a different place. I used to live in the same town too, but I moved away for ten years, and then came back again.

Report on question _____:

_____

_____

_____

_____

_____

Report on question _____:

_____

_____

_____

_____

_____

D Now choose one of these reports and read it to the rest of your class.

PART 2

Class talk

Think back to when you were a child. Tell the others about:
- a toy that you liked very much
- a person who you liked very much
- a place that you liked very much

20 Then and now

PART *1*

Vocabulary

What can you see here? Write the words next to the numbers below.

aeroplanepocketcalculatorcarphotocopiertelevisionpaperbackwatchtelephonefridge
washingmachineelectriclightbulbballpointpen

1 _____	5 _____	9 _____
2 *an aeroplane*	6 _____	10 _____
3 _____	7 _____	11 _____
4 _____	8 _____	12 _____

PART *2*

You and me

PARTNER *A*

■ Write a few words in the boxes about your past, and then change books
with your partner.

● a year that was important
to you

● a place that was important
to you

● a person who was
important to you

● something you saw that
you'll always remember

● your best decision

● your worst mistake

■ Have you got your partner's book now?
Ask your partner to tell you more about the things in his/her book.

You and me

PARTNER **B**

■ Write a few words in the boxes about your past, and then change books with your partner.

- a year that was important to you

- a place that was important to you

- a person who was important to you

- something you saw that you'll always remember

- your best decision

- your worst mistake

■ Have you got your partner's book now?
Ask your partner to tell you more about the things in his/her book.

PART **3**

Class talk

- Go back to Part 1. How important are those things to you? Number them 1–12 (1 = most important, 12 = least important). Compare your list with several other people in your class. Which does your class think is the most important and least important?
- How do you think your grandparents or your great-grandparents managed without these things? What did they have instead?

Holidays

PART 1

Opinions

These two people are very positive about their holidays:

My boyfriend and I always go on a package holiday. They're really the best holidays to take. It's so easy – you pay your money and everything is organised for you. You don't have to think about anything at all.

We go camping every summer. We get a lot of fresh air and can travel and stop where we want. There are five of us in the family, and so camping is much cheaper than other types of holidays.

Work with a partner to make a list of the possible disadvantages of camping holidays or package holidays. Then compare your list with others in your class.

PART 2

Holidays to remember

Work in groups of three or four. Tell the other people in your group about your last holiday or a holiday you remember because it was special. The others will ask you questions . . . but you could tell them about:
- the way you travelled
- where you stayed
- the things you liked most about the holiday

Give plenty of details.

Vocabulary

A Match these symbols from hotel descriptions with the words.

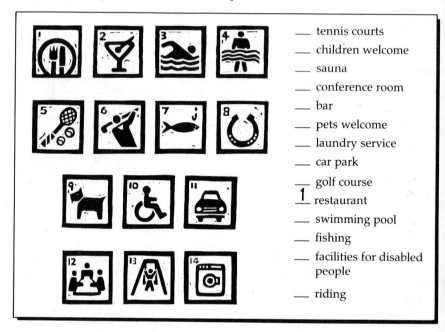

____ tennis courts

____ children welcome

____ sauna

____ conference room

____ bar

____ pets welcome

____ laundry service

____ car park

____ golf course

_1_ restaurant

____ swimming pool

____ fishing

____ facilities for disabled people

____ riding

B You want to book a hotel room, and you want the room to be very nice. Write five sentences about the room or hotel using *must*.
Example:

The hotel must be near the sea.
The room must have a balcony.

1 _____

2 _____

3 _____

4 _____

5 _____

Compare your list with others. How many different ideas are there in your class?

PART 4

Class talk

• What differences do you think there probably are in the types of holidays the following people enjoy?
  1 a single person aged 20
  2 a married couple with two young children
  3 a retired couple
• What are they looking for when they go on holiday?
• Collect all your comments together for the three categories.

Holidays

Vocabulary

Write words in here to show what you think can help to make a holiday good or bad. Try not to use any of the words more than once, and don't use the words *good* or *bad*.

Example:
Excellent, well-cooked and interesting food can help to make a holiday good. Cold, boring and badly-cooked food can help to make a holiday bad!

Good holiday		Bad holiday	
_____	food	_____	food
_____	hotel	_____	hotel
_____	weather	_____	weather
_____	people	_____	people
_____	scenery	_____	scenery

PART 2

You and me

PARTNER A

■ Make a list of five possible reasons why it's better for a family of four to travel a distance of 300 kilometres by car, and not by train.

1

2

3

4

5

■ Your partner has got a list of why it's better for a family to travel this distance by train. Compare your lists, and decide which *you* prefer.

■ **Interview your partner** Ask the questions below, and if he/she answers *yes*, continue the conversation with at least two more questions:

Example:
Have you ever been to North America? (Yes, I have.) When did you go there? Which part did you visit? Why . . .

Find out if he/she:
a) has ever been to North America, Canada or Australia
b) has ever been to a country with a very different culture from at home
c) has ever been to a country where the scenery is very different from at home
d) has ever been to a country without understanding the language at all
e) has ever gone abroad to learn a language or to work

■ Your partner has got some questions to ask you. Give plenty of information in your answers.

You and me

PART **2**

> ## PARTNER **B**
>
> ■ Make a list of five possible reasons why it's better for a family of four to travel a distance of 300 kilometres by train, and not by car.
>
> 1
> 2
> 3
> 4
> 5
>
> Your partner has got a list of five reasons why it is better for a family to travel this distance by car. Compare your lists and decide which *you* prefer.
>
> ■ Your partner has got some questions to ask you. Give plenty of information in your answers.
>
> ■ **Interview your partner**. Ask the questions below, and if he/she answers *yes*, continue the conversation with at least two more questions:
>
> *Example:*
> *Have you ever been camping? (Yes, I have.) Where did you camp? What was the weather like? What was the most difficult thing about camping? Did you . . .*
>
> Find out if he/she:
> 1) has ever been camping
> 2) has ever gone on holiday alone
> 3) has ever gone on a package holiday
> 4) has ever gone on holiday with a group of friends
> 5) has ever had a holiday that wasn't enjoyable

PART **3**

Class talk

Have you ever travelled in any of the following ways? Tell the others of the experiences you've had.

23 Health

PART 1

Pictures to talk about

A Some people might say that the people in these pictures are doing things that are bad for their health. Number these pictures 1 to 6, starting with what you think is the worst thing to do.

B Work with a partner to decide on one sentence for each picture beginning with *You shouldn't . . .*

Example: You shouldn't go to bed late every day.

1 You shouldn't _____

2 You shouldn't_____

3 You shouldn't _____

4 You shouldn't _____

5 You shouldn't _____

6 You shouldn't _____

Compare sentences with two other students.

C Perhaps it's just a question of doing these things too often or too much. Work in groups of three or four to decide what limits you could put on each of the activities in the pictures.

Example: Lying in the sun is okay, but not for the whole day.

Tips for health

Work in groups of three or four. Add nine more ideas to this list of golden rules for health. The list is for young people who are just starting their first jobs in offices.

Useful language:
Never (sit) . . .
Try to (sit) . . .
Avoid (sitting) . . .
Make a point of (sitting) . . .
Make sure you (sit) . . .
Don't (sit) . . .

GOLDEN RULES FOR YOUR HEALTH!

1 Try to walk for at least fifteen minutes on your way to and from work.

2

3

4

5

6

7

8

9

10

Compare your list with another group's list.

PART *3*

Class talk

- Which of these do you think are real health risks in your society?

  smoking   drinking alcohol   polluted air   chemicals   noise
  drugs and medicines   stress   other _____?

- Can you suggest ways of reducing these risks?
- Are there any other risks?

24 Health

Vocabulary

Label these parts of the body:

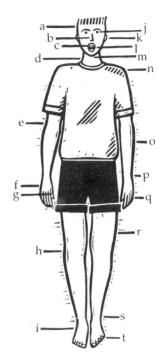

☐ finger	☐ nose
☐ head	☐ tooth
☐ shoulder	☐ hand
☐ eye	☐ wrist
☐ arm	☐ knee
☐ mouth	☐ thumb
☐ toe	☐ leg
☐ elbow	☐ ear
☐ chin	☐ neck
☐ ankle	☐ foot

Eighteen of these twenty words form the plural by adding 's'.
Which two don't add 's'? What are their plurals?

PART **2**

You and me

PARTNER **A**

■ Before you and your partner start the interview below, answer the
questions yourself with a tick (√) or a cross (×).

■ Interview your partner. Find out:

	Me	My partner
a) if he/she has ever broken a bone	____	____
b) if he/she has ever had an operation	____	____
c) if he/she has ever had an accident	____	____
d) if he/she has ever been in a hospital abroad (as a patient, visitor or to work)	____	____
e) if he/she has ever given up doing something for health reasons	____	____

■ Now answer your partner's questions.

■ Now go back over both interviews with your partner. There is a total of
ten questions. How many of these questions did you both answer with
yes and how many did you both answer with *no*?

■ If your partner answered *yes* to any of your questions above, ask
him/her to tell you more about what happened.

You and me

PARTNER **B**

■ Before your partner interviews you, answer the questions yourself in the interview below with a tick (√) or a cross (×).

■ Answer the questions that your partner has got for you.

■ Interview your partner. Find out:

	Me	My partner
1) if he/she has been to see a doctor this year	_____	_____
2) if he/she has been to see a dentist this year	_____	_____
3) if he/she has been ill this year	_____	_____
4) if he/she has had an accident this year	_____	_____
5) if he/she has been inside a hospital this year (as a patient, a visitor or to work)	_____	_____

■ Now go back over both interviews with your partner. There is a total of ten questions. How many of these questions did you both answer with *yes* and how many did you both answer with *no*?

■ If your partner answered *yes* to any of your questions above – ask him/her to tell you more about what happened.

PART **3**

Class talk

Divide your class into three groups. Each group should take one of the following topics:

relaxation   physical exercise   food and drink

● Discuss the things that you do that are good for you or bad for you. One person in each group should make notes so that he/she can report the comments of the group to the rest of the class.

● When the reports have been made, collect a list of the things that people in the class do that they know are (or could be) bad for their health.

● Do the people who do these things want to change? Have they tried to change?

Free time

A questionnaire

A This is the beginning of a questionnaire about entertainment. Work with two or three other people to add six more questions beginning with *Have you ever...?*

Some ideas: cinema (different kinds of films), circus, concert (different kinds of music), cabaret, pantomime, opera, theatre (different kinds of plays), to sing, to dance

Name					
1 Have you ever been to a pop music concert?					
2 Have you ever seen people making a film?					
3 Have you ever been inside a radio or television studio?					
4 Have you ever acted in a play?					
5					
6					
7					
8					
9					
10					

B Now ask these questions to five people – if possible they should be five people who didn't work on the questions with you. Fill in their answers with a tick (√) or a cross (✕).

C Choose two of the positive answers you got, go back to the people who gave them and ask two or three more questions.

For example, Anna answered *yes* to question 4, so you know that she has acted in a play at some time in her past. Now you can ask some more questions about that.

Example:
What was the name of the play? Where did you act in this play? How old were you at the time? Were you nervous? Did you find it difficult to learn your lines? Who were you in the play? What sort of play was it?

D Write the information you get in a short report like this:

Example:
Report on Anna's answer to question 4:

> Anna has acted in a play. She was fifteen years old at the time and the play was at her school. She didn't find it too difficult to learn the words because her mother helped her. She was a bit nervous on the first night.

Report on _____'s answer to question ___ :

_____
_____
_____
_____
_____
_____

Report on _____'s answer to question ___ :

_____
_____
_____
_____
_____
_____

E Now choose one of these reports and read it to the rest of your class.

PART 2

Class talk

Tell the others about:
- the type of entertainment you most enjoy
- any types of entertainment that you definitely don't like
- a film, play, concert, opera, musical, etc. that you have seen and that you remember very well

26 Free time

Vocabulary

A What hobbies do these people have? Write in the vowels to complete the words.

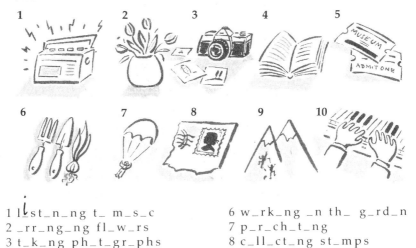

the vowels you need:

a a a a a a a a a
a a
e e e e e e e e
i i i i i i i i i i i i
i i i i i
o o o o o o o
u u u u

1 l i st_n_ng t_ m_s_c
2 _rr_ng_ng fl_w_rs
3 t_k_ng ph_t_gr_phs
4 r__d_ng
5 v_s_t_ng m_s__ms

6 w_rk_ng _n th_ g_rd_n
7 p_r_ch_t_ng
8 c_ll_ct_ng st_mps
9 cl_mb_ng
10 pl_y_ng th_ pi_n_

B Number these hobbies 1 to 10, starting with the one you think could interest you the most. Compare lists with a partner.

You and me

PARTNER A

■ **Interview your partner** Try to discover as much as you can about his/her free time. Find out:

a) what he/she usually does on Sundays
b) if he/she does any sports regularly (or used to do any sports regularly)
c) what sort of music he/she likes best, and what sort of reading material he/she usually chooses
d) how he/she spends a typical weekday (in detail, and including the free time)
e) what hobby or free time activity he/she would like to learn or take up (also find out why he/she hasn't done this up to now)

■ Your partner's got some questions to ask you. Give plenty of information in your answers.

■ Are televisions, cars and telephones positive or negative things for our free time? Make a list of at least two *positive* points for each thing. Now discuss these points with your partner (he/she has got a list of negative points). What changes have these things brought with them?

■ Make a group of four with your partner and another **A/B** pair. Compare your lists of positive and negative points.

You and me

PART *2*

PARTNER *B*

■ Your partner's got some questions to ask you. Give plenty of information in your answers.

■ Tell your partner to look at the list of hobbies in part one of this unit. Interview your partner. Ask:
1) which of these hobbies he/she has already tried
2) which of these hobbies he/she would definitely not like to try, and why
3) which of these hobbies he/she would like to try
4) if he/she finds any of these hobbies too dangerous, too expensive or too difficult to learn
5) what his/her favourite free time activity is

■ Are televisions, cars and telephones positive or negative things for our free time? Make a list of at least two *negative* points for each thing. Now discuss these points with your partner (he/she has got a list of positive points). What changes have these things brought with them?

■ Make a group of four with your partner and another **A/B** pair. Compare your lists of positive and negative points.

PART *3*

Class talk

• What do you think are the differences in the ways these people spend their free time?

• What is important to them at this point in their lives? What makes them choose to do some things and not to do others?

27 Plans for the future

PART 1

Future plans

A These two people have got some plans for the future.

" I'm going to look for a new job and a new flat next month. I'm going to look in the newspapers and ask all my friends for help. I'd like to move to another town, or go and live in the country. Anyway, I'm not going to stay where I am until this time next year – I know that. **"**

" I'm going to visit an old schoolfriend of mine next weekend. We're going to watch a football match on Saturday afternoon, but I don't know what we're going to do in the evening. On Sunday, we plan to stay at home until midday and then go to his parents' house for lunch. We're hoping to have a super lunch there. **"**

Work with a partner to write some interesting comments for the two people below. Use *going to*, *not going to*, *would like to*, *hoping to* and *plan to*.

" I'm going to retire next summer.
....
....
....
....
....
....
....
....
....
....
....
"

" We're going to build ourselves a house next year.
....
....
....
....
....
....
"

B Now one of you take the part of the man who is going to retire, and the other take the part of either the man or woman on the right. Tell the rest of the class about your plans for the future.

C Work in groups of three or four. Tell the other people in your group about some plans you've got for the future (if you haven't got any, you could invent some really exciting ones!). Talk about later today, tomorrow, next weekend, next year or even further into the future.

Useful language:
After the lesson
I'm going to . . .
I'm not going to . . .
Next weekend I'd like to . . .
Next year I plan to . . .
Next week I'm hoping to . . .

PART 2

The end of the course

Work in groups of about six to discuss the following problem. You'll need to make several suggestions so that the class will have a choice.

Your course is going to end in about five weeks' time. Make some plans for a weekend that you'd like to spend together. You don't want to spend *too* much money, but you'd like to include as much English as possible.

When you've got plans for the weekend, exchange them with other groups in your class and make a definite class decision about what you're going to do together.

Useful language:
Why don't we (go) . . .?
How about (going) . . .?
Shall we (go) . . .?
I suggest that we (go) . . .
We could (go) . . .

PART 3

Class talk

You're all going to live in a small, new country called Kazoonoland. This is the perfect moment for you to try and change the things you don't like in the society where you live now. Discuss:
- what you're going to do with criminals in your society
- how people are going to live and work in your society
- what your towns are going to be like
- what your schools and shops are going to be like

28 Plans for the future

Vocabulary

There are different types of plans that people can make. Match the types in box A with the contents of plans in box B.

A

1 itinerary
2 timetable
3 shopping list
4 appointments
5 budget
6 agenda
7 checklist

B

_____ the names of patients who are going to see the doctor next week

_____ the things that have to be discussed at a business meeting

_____ the things someone needs for a party

_____ the lessons for a class at school

_____ the important things you must do before leaving home for a few weeks

_____ the details of a business trip (hotels, flights, meetings, etc.)

_____ how you are going to spend your money next month

PART 2

You and me

PARTNER A

■ Before you start talking to your partner, choose the words you need to complete this story. Where you see '___' you can write in something yourself (try to use this line at least four times).

I'm going to have a holiday
☐ _____ ,
☐ later this year,
☐ next year,
and am going to spend
☐ _____
☐ 2 weeks
☐ a month

☐ _____ ,
☐ in France.
☐ in the USA.
I'm going to travel
☐ _____ .
☐ by plane.
☐ by car.

I'm going on holiday
☐ _____ ,
☐ alone,
☐ with a friend,
and I'm/we're going to stay
☐ _____ .
☐ in a hotel.
☐ with friends.

I'm/we're going to
☐ _____ .
☐ stay in one place all the time.
☐ travel around.

I usually send
☐ _____
☐ about 5
☐ between 5 and 15
postcards when I'm on holiday,

and I know I'm going to send one to
☐ _____
☐ my mother
☐ my neighbour
this time.

■ Now ask your partner questions so that you can mark the words that he/she has got in the story.
Example: When are you going to have a holiday?

■ Your partner is going to ask you the questions now. Only answer questions that you think are correct. If your partner asks an incorrect question, help him/her to correct it before you answer it.

■ In fours retell your partner's holiday plans to the group.

You and me

PARTNER **B**

■ Before you start talking to your partner, choose the words you need to complete this story. Where you see '___' you can write in something yourself (try to use this line at least four times).

I'm going to have a holiday

☐ ___,
☐ later this year,
☐ next year,

and am going to spend

☐ ___
☐ 2 weeks
☐ a month

☐ ___.
☐ in France.
☐ in the USA.

I'm going to travel

☐ ___.
☐ by plane.
☐ by car.

I'm going on holiday

☐ ___,
☐ alone,
☐ with a friend,

and I'm/we're going to stay

☐ ___.
☐ in a hotel.
☐ with friends.

I'm/we're going to

☐ ___.
☐ stay in one place all the time.
☐ travel around.

I usually send

☐ ___
☐ about 5
☐ between 5 and 15

postcards when I'm on holiday,

and I know I'm going to send one to

☐ ___
☐ my mother
☐ my neighbour

this time.

■ Your partner is going to ask you some questions now to find out which words you've got in your story. Only answer questions you think are correct. If your partner asks you an incorrect question, help him/her to correct it before you answer it.

■ Now ask your partner the questions so that you can mark the words that he/she has got in the story.
Example: When are you going to have a holiday?

■ In fours retell your partner's holiday plans to the group.

Class talk

Do you think it's a good idea to plan for the future?
What things do you need to plan for:
- a party you're going to give next weekend?
- your immediate future (the next few months)?
- your holiday in six months' time?
- the more distant future (five years from now or when you retire)?

Answer key

1 1A: 1c, 2a, 3d, 4b

2 1: 1 baker's 2 butcher's 3 chemist's 4 florist's 5 stationer's 6 greengrocer's 7 grocer's

4 1A: tennis court: ball, racket, net
golf course: ball, club, hole
badminton court: shuttlecock, racket, net
hockey field: ball, stick, goal

B: hockey

2: the differences: a) female referee/male referee b) two women playing/woman and man playing c) press photographer/no press photographer d) one ball on ground by net/no balls on ground e) no ballboy next to referee/ballboy next to referee f) sun shining/cloudy g) scoreboard shows 3:2/scoreboard shows 2:1 h) one cup on table/two cups on table

5 1A: 1b, 2c, 3a, 4d

2: Anna's part is numbered:
3, 8, 1, 5, 9, 6, 4, 2, 7

6 1: 1 window 2 roof 3 upstairs 4 door 5 attic 6 stairs 7 wall 8 chimney 9 downstairs
a) chimney b) roof c) window d) wall e) door f) attic g) upstairs h) stairs i) downstairs

7 1A: 1d 2a 3e 4b 5f 6c

8 2: the differences: 1 calendar on wall/picture on wall 2 flowers in vase/plant in pot 3 computer on desk/typewriter on desk 4 view of trees through window/view of buildings through window 5 picture of woman on desk/picture of children on desk 6 wastebin under desk/wastebin beside desk 7 swivel chair/four-legged chair 8 two telephones/one telephone 9 four books scattered on desk/three books in a pile on desk 10 cup and saucer on desk/glass on desk

9 1A: 1c 2a 3d 4b

10 1: the food: interesting, awful, over-cooked, excellent
the service: slow, friendly, unfriendly, fast
the inside: attractive, modern, elegant, shabby

11 2: 1 coins 2 cheque 3 note 4 credit card coins, notes

12 1: dollars: Australia, Canada, USA, New Zealand, Singapore
francs: Belgium, Congo, France, Luxembourg, Switzerland
pesos: Bolivia, Columbia, Cuba, Mexico, Philippines
pounds: Britain, Cyprus, Egypt, Gibraltar, Malta

13 3A: hair: 3, 1, 2 nose: 2, 3, 1 face: 3, 1, 2 other: 2, 1, 3

14 1: 1 small 2 narrow 3 short 4 light 5 special 6 elegant 7 cheap 8 modern

16 1A: female: cousin, daughter-in-law, sister-in-law, granddaughter, mother-in-law, wife, mother, niece, aunt, grandmother, daughter, sister
male: brother, cousin, uncle, son, grandfather, father-in-law, brother-in-law, son-in-law, grandson, husband, nephew, father

18 1A: 1 history 2 French 3 physics 4 music 5 English 6 mathematics 7 geography, 8 chemistry 9 cookery 10 computer

20 1A: 1 a fridge 2 an aeroplane 3 a light bulb 4 a watch 5 a telephone 6 a television 7 a ballpoint pen 8 a paperback 9 a washing machine 10 a calculator 11 a photocopier 12 a car

21 3A: 1 restaurant 2 bar 3 swimming pool 4 sauna 5 tennis courts 6 golf course 7 fishing 8 riding 9 pets welcome 10 facilities for disabled people 11 car park 12 conference room 13 children welcome 14 laundry service

24 1:

a) head	f) hand	k) ear	p) wrist
b) nose	g) thumb	l) mouth	q) finger
c) tooth	h) knee	m) chin	r) leg
d) neck	i) foot	n) shoulder	s) ankle
e) arm	j) eye	o) elbow	t) toe

tooth/teeth, foot/feet

26 1: 1) listening to music 2) arranging flowers 3) taking photographs 4) reading 5) visiting museums 6) working in the garden 7) parachuting 8) collecting stamps 9) climbing 10) playing the piano

28 1: 4 6 3 6 2 7 1 5

Longman Group UK Limited,
Longman House, Burnt Mill, Harlow,
Essex CM20 2JE, England
and Associated Companies throughout the world.

© Longman Group UK Limited 1989

First published 1989
Seventh impression 1992

Set in 9/11pt Palatino
Produced by Longman Singapore Publishers (Pte) Ltd
Printed in Singapore

ISBN 0-582-00299-0

Acknowledgements
The publishers would like to thank all those involved in
reporting and advising on this material in its draft stages.
Also, all those UK schools involved in the pilot study of the
Longman Skills series:

LONDON: International House; Central School; Davies
School; Kingsway Princeton
CAMBRIDGE: Eurocentre; Anglo-World; Cambridge
Academy
EDINBURGH: Stevenson College; Basil Paterson;
Edinburgh Language Foundation;
EASTBOURNE: English Centre
TORQUAY: Torquay International
OXFORD: Godmer House; Swan School; Anglo-World
BRIGHTON: Regent School; St Giles' School
BOURNEMOUTH: Anglo-Continental; BEET Language
Centre; English Language Centre
HASTINGS: International House; EF International School
EXETER: International School

We are grateful to the following for permission to
reproduce illustrative material in this book:

AGE FOTOStock for pages 7 (bottom left) and 31 (top
right and bottom right); Barnabys Picture Library/Rudy
Lewis for page 7 (top left); The J Allan Cash Photolibrary
for page 31 (top left); Dillons The Bookstore for pages 9
and 10; Robert Harding Picture Library for page 15
(bottom); The Hutchison Library for page 15 (top centre);
Longman Photographic Unit for pages 20 and 23 (bottom
left); Longman Photographic Unit/St John Pope for pages
29 and 30; Network Photographers for page 23 (top left);
Our Price Records for page 7 (top right); Picturepoint
Limited for pages 23 (bottom right) and 58 (middle);
Tony Stone Photo Library – London for pages 7 (bottom
right), 15 (top left and top right), 31 (bottom left) and 58
(left and right); Trusthouse Forte (UK) Limited for page
23 (top right).

Illustrated by Nancy Anderson, Ray Burrows, Andrew
Harris, Norah Kenna, Francis Lloyd, Karl Mather and
Stephen Wright.